THE GIRL WITH A 100 MILE AN HOUR BRAIN

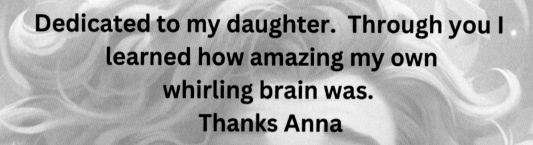

Dedicated to my daughter. Through you I
learned how amazing my own
whirling brain was.
Thanks Anna

THE GIRL
WITH A 100
MILE AN
HOUR BRAIN

Notes For Parents

I hope you find this book useful – if I had read it when I was younger it would have been hugely helpful. I would have known that I was not the only person in the world who thought the way I did, I would have known that I was not just "inherently naughty," as my teachers described me and instead, I had a gift that they had failed to recognize.

I didn't know I had ADHD until my own daughter was diagnosed with it. My parents and friends were saying things like "She's just a chip off the old block," and I too thought she was indeed just like me and struggled the same way at school. The sessions she had to help her with ADHD were as helpful to me as they were to her.

It was a lightbulb moment when I found out why I fidgeted and struggled to focus during lessons and lectures. And it very well might be that while you are reading this you may also think " Hey - I do that?" and "I've felt that that as well."

I'm not going to go into a detailed description here of the types of ADHD and the varying strategies used to get the best out of ourselves here, that's not the purpose of this book. My reason for writing this is to reach out to you and to your child and say "Good for You." This is a gift, you've just got to learn how to use it. You need to ignore people who use the ADHD label as an excuse for bad behaviour, and ignore those who think that you'll amount to nothing because you have some "mental condition" that will prevent you from succeeding.

All this is totally wrong.

I finished school and college and graduated with a first-class law degree. Not too shabby for someone with ADHD. I've started my own businesses, run international exhibitions, fronted talks and seminars and written fiction and non-fiction books. I attribute my success to ADHD.

If asked I tell people ADHD is my superpower.

My brain hardly ever shuts down, it's always crammed with ideas. When I have a problem my brain processes it over and over again, sometimes for hours sometimes for days until I finalise a solution. I don't give in and why should I when I can think of a way forward, a successful way forward.

Stopping thinking can be the problem. Finding sleep sometimes when the computer in my head is whirling and crunching possibilities can be a challenge. But it is a small price to pay for the ability to be able to think at speed!

Olivia liked school - most of the time. She liked playtime, especially when it was sunny and the sports box came out. Then there were skipping ropes, balls, and hopscotch to play. She had two friends, Alice and Henry, and Olivia was always thinking up games for them to play. One day they'd be playing heroes and villains, hide and seek or she would have marked out a new hopscotch route in chalk on the playground. Every day was different.

What wasn't too different though were the lessons! Olivia didn't mind art, that was okay, usually. Sometimes they would paint, sometimes it would be drawing and sometimes they would make things.

Olivia liked these lessons best, making things out of paper, cardboard, string and glue was what she did best. Today they made a robot. Olivia didn't get bored once. Each part of the robot was a different task. Making the legs, cutting out the arms, finding a good box to make the head, and glueing on the milk carton lids for the eyes.

The next lesson was English. Olivia could feel energy draining from her as she sat down at her desk and got out her book.

The teacher, Mrs Potter, was telling them they were going to be working on a piece of descriptive writing about a snake. They had to think of different ways to describe the snake, thinking about texture and feel and colour.

Mrs Potter went on and on ….. Olivia knew she was stopping listening to Mrs Potter, she tried to, but it was too hard.

Olivia had already thought of some great words to describe her snake who she had decided to call George, and finding her pen began to write them down.

Scaly

Green Beady-eyed

Hissing

Reaching over she pulled a green pencil from the pen pot and started to draw a picture of George in her book. As she drew him she decided George wasn't going to be any old snake, he was going to be a snake monster. She gave him a huge fat belly lots of scales, a curly tail and feet. Olivia knew snakes didn't have feet but snake monsters probably would, and George definitely looked better with feet.

"Olivia?" Mrs Potter said very loudly.

She didn't hear her name being called and continued to colour in George's scales.

"Olivia?"

Getting a yellow crayon she coloured in the snake's eyes.

"Olivia!!"

Olivia jumped, and everyone else in the class laughed. Mrs Potter was standing right behind her.

"What have you done to your book?" Mrs Potter sounded furious, and taking her book held it up for the rest of the class to see.

"Snakes don't have legs," Jeered Charlie Thomas from the back of the class.

"And they aren't that shape either," laughed Emily Parsons.

The class laughed even more and Olivia felt her eyes filling with tears.

Shortly afterwards Olivia found herself outside the Principal's office with her English book on her knee. It was closed and she didn't want to open it and look at the picture of George that had got her in trouble.

Mr Jones was the Principal and he smiled when he opened the door. "Come on in, Olivia."

Olivia went in and sat down, there was a phone on the desk and she really hoped Mr Jones wasn't going to use it to ring her parents.

They would be so upset if she was in trouble again. Last term they had got a phone call when she had been in trouble for shouting loudly in class and another when she had told jokes to her friends during assembly. She didn't mean to be disruptive, it just happened sometimes.

Olivia couldn't help herself and glanced at the phone again.

Mr Jones smiled. "Don't worry, you're not in trouble."

Olivia looked up confused. Pupils only ever came to the Principal's office when they were in trouble.

"Let me have a look at your book," Mr Jones held out his hand and Olivia slowly passed him the book. He turned the pages until he found the picture of George and the list of words she'd written.

"Mrs Potter said you started to write in your book before she'd finished telling you what to do?" Mr Jones said.

Olivia shrugged. "She'd told us what to do, and I guess just started a bit quickly."

"What did she tell you she wanted you to do?" Mr Jones asked.

"She wanted us to describe a snake, and come up with a list of good words to use in a poem so I did that," Olivia explained.

"Did she tell you to draw a picture in your English book?" Mr Jones asked.

Olivia shook her head. "I'd already made my list of words, so I just wanted something else to do."

"You made a good list, and you did that really quickly," Mr Jones said, he sounded pleased, then asked, "How did you manange to do it so quickly?"

"The words just appear in my head all at the same time. So I just wrote them down. And I could see pictures of snakes and I decided to draw one, but then I thought a snake-monster would be more fun. That's why I added the legs, and everyone laughed at me."

"You wrote a good list of words, Olivia, and I think Mrs Potter was just annoyed that you were working and ignoring her while she was still talking," Mr Jones said.

"I guess so," Olivia said, glancing again at the phone on the desk.

"I think I'd like you to see Miss Kelly. She comes to school twice a week to help students like you. And I think she might be able to stop you from getting into trouble with Mrs Potter again," Mr Jones said closing her book and handing back to her.

"I'm not in trouble?" Olivia said nervously.

"Not at all," Mr Jones said, standing up. "When Miss Kelly is next in school she'll come and find out and you can have a chat about how you find your lessons."

It was two days later when Olivia met Miss Kelly. She came looking for her just after playtime and they went back to Miss Kelly's room which was not far from the Principal's office.

Olivia had thought it would be like the Principal's office with a big desk, chairs and shelves with books but it wasn't at all like that. Miss Kelly had a sofa and lots of books. On the wall were large coloured pictures of children playing on the beach.

"It's a great picture," Miss Kelly said, "it makes me feel really relaxed. Sometimes when I'm sitting on the sofa I can just imagine myself walking on the sandy beach."

Miss Kelly explained that Olivia wasn't in trouble at all, but she just wanted to know what happened in her classes sometimes.

Olivia told her that sometimes, when she got bored, she would stare out of the window, and stop paying attention, or start thinking about new games she was going to play with her friends in the playground. Mrs Potter would say "Olivia you've zoned out again!"

Olvia then told Miss Kelly that sometimes she got into trouble for shouting out answers in class. She couldn't help herself, and the words just came out, usually quite loud. The teachers were always saying "Give some of the other children a chance," or "Olivia, please wait until I pick you."

Miss Kelly asked Olivia about what had happened in Mrs Potter's class. Olivia explained that Mrs Potter had told the class over and over what she wanted them to do and Olivia had just wanted to get 'get on with it'.

She'd already worked out what her list of words were going to be and then knew exactly what a snake looked like so she'd stopped listening to Mrs Potter and started writing and drawing instead.

Miss Kelly asked if Olivia often had difficulty listening in class?

Olivia explained that it was fine to start with but once she knew what she had to do she always got impatient and wanted to start. If the teachers talked for a long time she often started to look out of the classroom window to see what was happening outside and then she'd get in trouble for not paying attention. Or she'd start to draw pictures in her workbook or talk to her friend Will who sat next to her. Sometimes she just thought about what she was going to do after school finished, like taking her dog for a walk.

Miss Kelly seemed to understand and didn't think this was a bad thing at all, which made Olivia feel a lot better. She always hated getting into trouble in class.

Miss Kelly asked her what she liked best about school.

Olivia told her about playtime when she invented new games for her friends each day which they enjoyed. Then she told Miss Kelly about the art class when she had been making a robot and had found that easy to do. Miss Kelly asked her why she had found it easy and enjoyable.

Olivia explained that making the model had been like doing lots of different things rather than one long task. Making the head, making the legs, cutting out the arms had all been different things to do and she'd found it easy to finish the task. Sometimes, Olivia told Miss Kelly, she got distracted and found herself looking out of the window, or talking to her friends and then she didn't get her classwork finished.

Miss Kelly seemed to understand Olivia's problems and said, "You are very lucky, Olivia, your brain is wired up differently than most people's, it means that you can think faster, and often think about lots of things at the same time. My name is actually Dr Kelly and I specialise in helping people like you."

Olivia frowned. "You don't look like a Doctor?"

Miss Kelly laughed. "I try not to, otherwise you'll think you are going to get a shot and you'll worry about it."

"That's true," Olivia said. "I hate shots."

Miss Kelly got a workbook out that was full of puzzles and things to do, even blank pages for drawing pictures, and helped Olivia to get started. There were lots of different activities and Olivia didn't get bored at all.

"I can help you with getting your brain organised and helping you to focus on one thing at a time. I know your head probably feels like it's packed full of ideas at the same time and you can't choose what to focus on, or which is the right task for that moment, but I can certainly help you. Your brain runs faster than everyone else's, you are really lucky. I know it seems hard, and the thoughts inside your head often feel like you are caught in the middle of a tornado, but don't worry, I can help you control them," Miss Kelly said.

Olivia laughed. "That's exactly what it feels like sometimes. Mrs Potter says I always do naughty things, and I don't mean to, but how can you stop me?"

"Well," said Miss Kelly, "let's talk about when you drew George the snake. You told me you'd heard enough from Miss Potter and knew what you had to do, but she still hadn't finished telling the other children about the task. When this happens just getting up and leaving the room and walking to get a drink can help,"

"Miss Potter isn't going to let me leave her class whenever I want to," Olivia protested.

"She will do, it'll help you and the rest of the class as well," Miss Kelly explained.

Miss Kelly produced two coloured cards and told Olivia that these were hers to keep. Each one had a different purpose and her teachers would know that as well. So if she put the blue one on her desk she would be able to get up quietly, leave Mrs Potter's class and walk to the water fountain. Then when she came back she'd be able to sit down and start on the work.

There was a yellow card, and Miss Kelly showed Olivia how to do some simple breathing exercises to help her focus her mind. "When you put this card on the table your teacher will know you are working hard to get yourself back on task and focus and they'll know that and won't interrupt you. The card is saying to your teachers, I am trying hard to get back to my lesson."

"It sounds like a good idea," Olivia said picking up the two cards.

"This is just a start," Miss Kelly said, "We'll meet up regularly and I can help you out with any problems and I can teach you lots more ways to help you make the most of your super speedy brain."

Olivia was a bit nervous about the coloured cards, but she didn't need to be. Her teachers already knew about them and told her that whenever she needed to use them to just put them on the desk.

Over the next weeks Miss Kelly showed Olivia lots more techniques and told her about lots of famous people who also had ADHD like Albert Einstein and Bill Gates.

Olivia looked forward to her meetings with Miss Kelly and when the end of the year came and it was time for tests Olivia got the highest marks she'd ever had in Miss Potter's English class.

The End

Check out the great workbook like the one Olivia used for some great puzzles and info on ADHD Available on Amazon - ADHD Superpower Workbook by JJ McBridge

Made in the USA
Las Vegas, NV
09 May 2024

89717953R00017